CREATING DATA VISUALIZATIONS

DATA GEEK

KRISTIN FONTICHIARO

Published in the United States of America by Cherry Lake Publishing
Ann Arbor, Michigan
www.cherrylakepublishing.com

Series Adviser: Kristin Fontichiaro

Photo Credits: Cover and page 1, ©bleakstar/Shutterstock; page 5, ©Elena Elisseeva/Dreamstime.com; page 8, Florence Nightingale; page 12, ©Rawpixel.com/Shutterstock; page 15, Mikael Häggström/Wikimedia; pages 18, 24, and 28, Kristin Fontichiaro; page 20, Altes/Wikimedia; page 26, MartinThoma/Wikimedia

Library of Congress Cataloging-in-Publication Data
Names: Fontichiaro, Kristin, author.
Title: Creating data visualizations / by Kristin Fontichiaro.
Description: Ann Arbor, Michigan : Cherry Lake Publishing, [2017] |
Series: Data geek | Includes bibliographical references and index.
Identifiers: LCCN 2017001610 | ISBN 9781634727099 (lib. bdg.) |
    ISBN 9781634727426 (pbk.) | ISBN 9781634727754 (pdf) | ISBN 9781634728089
    (ebook)
Subjects: LCSH: Information visualization--Juvenile literature. | Visual
    analytics--Juvenile literature.
Classification: LCC QA76.9.I52 F66 2017 | DDC 001.4/226--dc23 LC record
available at https://lccn.loc.gov/2017001610

Cherry Lake Publishing would like to acknowledge the work of the Partnership for 21st Century Learning.
Please visit *www.p21.org* for more information.

Printed in the United States of America
Corporate Graphics

ABOUT THE AUTHOR

Kristin Fontichiaro helps librarians, educators, and kids develop data literacy skills, with funding made possible in part by the Institute of Museum and Library Services.

TABLE OF CONTENTS

CHAPTER 1

What Is Data Visualization? 4

CHAPTER 2

Getting Started 10

CHAPTER 3

Visualizing with Pie Charts 14

CHAPTER 4

Maps 19

CHAPTER 5

Bar Charts 25

FOR MORE INFORMATION..31
GLOSSARY 32
INDEX... 32

What Is Data Visualization?

Data visualization is all around us. It's a map in your social studies book showing which states fought on which side of the Civil War. It's a **pie chart** in math class or an **infographic** on social media. It's a **bar chart** hanging on the wall in a bank. Wherever you look, you're bound to spot some form of data visualization.

What is data? It's information. Specifically, data usually means numbers. Data visualization puts those numbers in an eye-catching visual format. Instead of just showing a boring list of numbers, visualizations organize and sort information into patterns that help you understand an issue.

You may have heard of the famous nurse Florence Nightingale. But did you know that she was a pioneer of data visualization?

You may have worked with data visualizations as part of your math assignments.

She wanted to show government and military leaders how many soldiers were dying unnecessarily. Take a look at the image on page 8, a close-up of part of her creation. You'll notice a circle divided into sections that each represent a month. Big events such as war efforts in Bulgaria and the Crimea are noted on the edge of certain months. Each month's pie slice is divided into additional sections. The farther out each pie slice reaches from the center, the more soldiers died that month. Nightingale's **key** (not shown here) identified the color scheme:

- **Red segments** represent the number of deaths because of wounds. Among warring soldiers, this kind of death was, sadly, to be expected. You can see that some months had many deaths from wounds because there is a greater amount of pink in those months.
- **Black segments** note death from other causes that are not specified.
- But it is the **blue segments** that really stand out. Those, Nightingale argued, were the number of soldiers who died of preventable diseases. In other words, these are the groups that did not need to die.

Graphics told the story much better than the numbers could have. Because the blue/gray portions take over the page,

Nightingale made her point. This introduces an important guideline to keep in mind as you create your own visualizations: Behind every visualization is someone making an argument. Nightingale's argument was that too many soldiers were dying unnecessarily. This weakened England's military strength, tied up too many medical workers, and cost too much money.

Today, you are more likely to see or make a chart or **graph** than a shape like Nightingale's. You're especially likely to gather a bunch of little visual bits of information together in an infographic.

Rule of Thumb for Visualizations

- *Use a visualization to add value and improve meaning. Don't create a visualization just to make something pretty.*
- *Label everything in a visualization.*
- *Every good visualization has a message behind it, even if it isn't said out loud.*

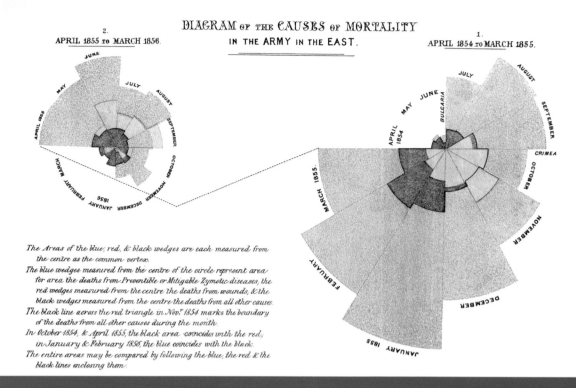

IN THE ARMY IN THE EAST.

2.
APRIL 1855 TO MARCH 1856.

1.
APRIL 1854 TO MARCH 1855.

The Areas of the blue, red, & black wedges are each measured from
the centre as the common vertex.
The blue wedges measured from the centre of the circle represent area
for area the deaths from Preventible or Mitigable Zymotic diseases, the
red wedges measured from the centre the deaths from wounds, & the
black wedges measured from the centre the deaths from all other causes.
The black line across the red triangle in Nov.r 1854 marks the boundary
of the deaths from all other causes during the month.
In October 1854, & April 1855, the black area coincides with the red,
in January & February 1856, the blue coincides with the black.
The entire areas may be compared by following the blue, the red & the
black lines enclosing them.

Florence Nightingale used graphics to convince others of
how many soldiers were dying unnecessarily.

In this book, we'll look at how we can gather data and then
use it to communicate information in a way that is clear,
meaningful, and valuable. We'll use simple data and the most
common visualization styles to get you started.

[21ST CENTURY SKILLS LIBRARY]

Visualizations from the Past

Today, we live in a visual world. Data visualizations are far more common than they were when your grandparents were young. However, visualizations are not new. The earliest visualizations looked a lot like drawings. Ancient Egyptian **hieroglyphs** could communicate valuable information through simple, hand-drawn symbols. Some pictures might communicate the amount of crops being grown or the number of workers required to carry out certain activities. Similarly, ancient cave paintings found in many parts of the world may have helped our ancestors keep track of how many animals they owned or hunted.

CHAPTER 2

Getting Started

Before you start, you need some data. You can't visualize information if you don't have any! Here are some common ways that students gather data.

Science Experiments

Science class is probably where you use the word *data* the most. Maybe you are doing a Science Olympiad egg drop challenge. In that case, you might collect three kinds of data: how long it takes for the egg to reach the ground (measured in seconds), the height from which the egg is dropped (measured in feet or meters), and how many eggs survived the drop. In another experiment, you might measure how much water evaporated over 10 minutes of high heat (measured in ounces or milliliters). You might also do simple counting. For example, in a lesson on genetics, you might find out how many of your classmates have certain genetic traits, such as blue eyes or the ability to curl one's tongue.

Social Studies

Social studies textbooks are a rich source of data, as well. Common data you run into in social studies or history class include the following:

- Population by city, state, or region; by gender; by ethnic group; by income level; or by education level (sorted into categories)
- Votes for presidential candidates (sorted into categories)
- Sizes of states or countries (measured in square miles or square kilometers)

Online Sources

Many times, when you need to visualize data, you'll be doing it for a class project. Want to find data on how many farmers

Rule of Thumb

Know what you are counting! This will help you get ideas for how to visualize your message later.

You might go online to collect data for a social studies project at school.

there are in each U.S. state? What percentage of Chinese citizens completed college? How much money U.S. stores make on Black Friday? You can find this kind of information in textbooks, newspapers, or nonfiction library books. You can also search online at government Web sites and other sources.

Surveys

One classic place for students to start doing visualizations is by asking some survey questions and visualizing that data. Think about questions you can sort into categories. "Do you like ice cream?" "How many pets do you have?" "Do you have a dog?" These kinds of questions are all examples of easy survey questions we can ask. They are easy to count up and graph. We'll use survey data in the rest of this book.

Got your data? Great! Let's look at ways to visualize it.

Finding Data Online

It may not be until you reach high school that you need to find data online. When you do, here are some good places to start. You might want to ask an adult at home, a librarian, or your teacher for help figuring out which data is best for your project.

- **U.S. Census American Fact Finder** (https://factfinder .census.gov/faces/nav/jsf/pages/index.xhtml) *is a good source for data on U.S. population, incomes, and communities.*
- **Data.gov** (www.data.gov) *is the U.S. government's main source for data of all kinds.*
- **The World Factbook** (https://www.cia.gov/library/publications /resources/the-world-factbook/index.html) *is the U.S. Central Intelligence Agency's source for data about size, population, income, and more for countries around the world.*
- **The World Bank** (data.worldbank.org) *is useful for international data about poverty and other global issues.*
- **Wolfram Alpha** (www.wolframalpha.com) *is a search engine that loves looking for data.*

CHAPTER 3

Visualizing with Pie Charts

One of the easiest visualizations to make is a pie chart. Pie charts are exactly what they sound like: visualizations shaped like pies. They are circles divided into "slices." Each slice is a different color or pattern. The bigger the group represented by the slice, the bigger the slice is.

Take a look at the pie chart on page 15 showing the population of each U.S. state. There's a lot going on here, because the pie chart is trying to represent each of the 50 states. If you look at a large state such as California (shown at 1:00, if you imagine the chart as a clock), it's easy to see how many people live there. But what if you want to know about New Hampshire? Its population isn't large enough to show up as a labeled slice. This isn't very

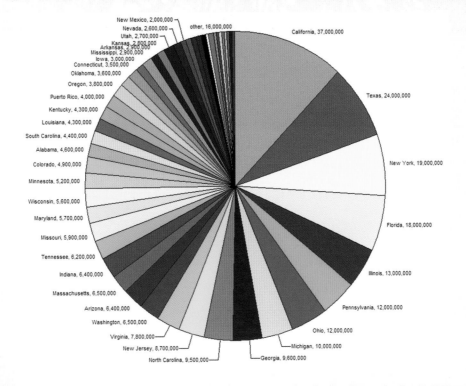

New Mexico, 2,000,000
Nevada, 2,600,000
Utah, 2,700,000
Kansas, 2,800,000
Arkansas, 2,900,000
Mississippi, 2,900,000
Iowa, 3,000,000
Connecticut, 3,500,000
Oklahoma, 3,600,000
Oregon, 3,800,000
Puerto Rico, 4,000,000
Kentucky, 4,300,000
Louisiana, 4,300,000
South Carolina, 4,400,000
Alabama, 4,600,000
Colorado, 4,900,000
Minnesota, 5,200,000
Wisconsin, 5,600,000
Maryland, 5,700,000
Missouri, 5,900,000
Tennessee, 6,200,000
Indiana, 6,400,000
Massachusetts, 6,500,000
Arizona, 6,400,000
Washington, 6,500,000
Virginia, 7,800,000
New Jersey, 8,700,000
North Carolina, 9,500,000
Georgia, 9,600,000
Michigan, 10,000,000
Ohio, 12,000,000
Pennsylvania, 12,000,000
Illinois, 13,000,000
Florida, 18,000,000
New York, 19,000,000
Texas, 24,000,000
California, 37,000,000
other, 16,000,000

Some types of data do not work well with pie charts.
This one is too cluttered and complicated.

helpful! To avoid this problem in your pie charts, try not to use so many categories.

Let's try making our own pie chart. Imagine asking a homeroom of 35 students, "Are you left-handed, right-handed, or can you switch between both hands?" Each student can only fit in one of these three categories. This is important for pie charts: You can only count each item a single time.

Here are the results. Out of 35 students, 10 were left-handed, 24 were right-handed, and one was able to use both hands equally well (this is called being ambidextrous). We call these raw numbers. They count the actual number of people who fit each category. Let's convert these numbers into percentages. This will help us know how big a slice each category should get.

- 35 students in class
- 10 left-handed (10 divided by 35 = 29%)
- 24 right-handed (24 divided by 35 = 69%)
- 1 ambidextrous (1 divided by 35 = 3%)

To make a pie chart, draw a circle and divide it up into sections that are about the right size. Remember that 25 percent is

Sketch It Out

It's tempting to grab some data and then use a fancy online tool or software to make it look great. But remember our Rule of Thumb: We want the look of our visualization to add strength to our data, not overwhelm it. Drawing by hand helps you know in advance what a computer-generated chart should look like. This can help you master the basics of good visualization. Later, when you move to digital visualization tools, you'll know enough to be in charge of your data. You won't have to rely on the computer to make decisions for you. When you have mastered drawing visualizations by hand, you can move to programs such as Microsoft Excel or online tools such as Google Sheets to make polished visualizations.

one-quarter of the pie and 50 percent is half the pie. Estimate other sizes from there.

Check the sample pie chart on page 18 against this checklist:

☐ Does the visualization have a title? (Yes: "Handedness in Room 109")

☐ Do we know the total number of items represented in the chart? (Yes: 35 students are listed under the title)

☐ Do we list the source of our data and the date of that data? (Yes: see the bottom-left corner)

☐ Is each pie slice a **distinct** color? (Yes)

☐ Is each slice labeled, either inside or outside, with the percentage, the raw number, and what is being counted? (Sometimes, instead of writing the words "left-handed" next to that slice, designers make a key at the bottom of the chart that matches the color used with the items counted in that slice. Either approach is fine as long as everything is labeled.)

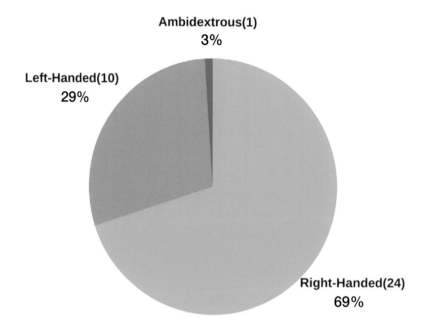

Handedness in Room 109
35 Students Total

Ambidextrous(1)
3%

Left-Handed(10)
29%

Right-Handed(24)
69%

Data gathered by class survey: September 22, 2017

Sometimes, we round numbers up or down to put them in a pie chart. That is what happened here. 29% + 69% + 3% = 101%. If the numbers add up to 99%, that's also OK. It just gives you a hint that the chart creator did not use fractions or decimals and rounded up or down instead.

Rules of Thumb for Pie Charts

- Use pie charts only when everything you are counting gets counted once.
- Bigger slices represent a bigger share of the whole.
- If you have too many categories, pie charts can be confusing. Try to keep them under 12 sections.
- Use different colors to set sections apart from one another.
- Label the pie chart with a title and the percentage for each slice.

CHAPTER 4

Maps

Maps are great for visualizing data when location is important. For example, when there is a presidential election, newscasters use maps to show which states are won by Democrats (blue) and Republicans (red).

You can also use colors to show how much of something there is in a certain location. The world map on page 20 shows the 2013 unemployment rate in each country.

Notice the colors in the key to the left. It shows how colors move from green to yellow, then orange, red, and dark red, as the percentage of people who are unemployed rises. The southern tip of Africa is dark red, meaning the unemployment rate measured there was 25 to 30 percent. What about the United States? Not perfect, but better than most countries: 5 to 10 percent unemployment. Notice

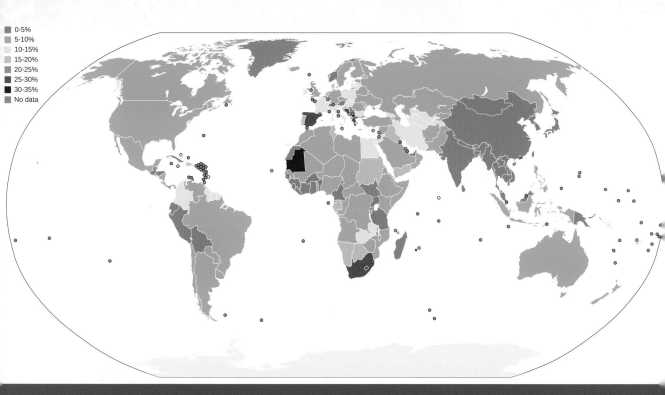

0-5%
5-10%
10-15%
15-20%
20-25%
25-30%
30-35%
No data

Notice how colors make it easy to see where unemployment is highest and lowest around the world.

how color helps communicate meaning. We instinctively see green as a good color. Green is the color of plants and money. Red is often used to mean negative things. It is the color of blood and anger. It makes sense that countries with better employment are marked with green and those where it is worse are marked with red.

Another way to use colors on a map is to pick one color. Let's use purple, for example. The boxes in the key would range from very light purple to very dark purple. Each shade of purple would be labeled as a percentage of unemployment. The lighter the purple, the less unemployment there is in an area.

[21ST CENTURY SKILLS LIBRARY]

Color Is a Powerful Tool!

It sounds weird, but color is powerful. It triggers an emotional reaction. Think about it. Which seems more serious: a red stop sign or a baby blue one? Which uniform color seems more commanding: navy blue or lavender?

Keep this in mind when planning your colors for a visualization. Sometimes, using the wrong colors can actually confuse our brains. Imagine a visualization where pink represented males and blue represented females. It's the opposite of what we are used to. Color is actually so powerful that it can make us reverse the data in our heads!

When making a map like this, you need to make sure that each shade is distinct so you can tell which purple is being used in each area. You should be able to figure out right away where the largest percentages of out-of-work people are when you glance at the map. Use gray sections to show where there was no data collected. Gray tells viewers that you thought about every part of the map and didn't just leave a bunch of areas blank!

Let's try making a map showing where each sixth grader in a class (150 in all) was born. This is a good question for a map visualization because each person can only be born in one place!

Surveys showed: 20 students born in Michigan, 19 in Wisconsin, 18 in New York, 16 in Indiana, 15 in Ohio, 12 in Washington, 11 in North Carolina, 10 in California, 10 in Nevada, 5 in Oregon, 4 in Illinois, 4 in South Carolina, 3 in Pennsylvania, 2 in Florida, 1 in North Dakota, and no one from any other state.

Take a look at the numbers in the list. What number ranges do we need in our key? We don't have any numbers higher than 20, so that can be our deepest color. Let's go down from there and make a key like this:

- 16–20
- 11–15
- 6–10
- 1–5
- none

Rules of Thumb for Maps

- *Using color ranges, such as a rainbow or several shades of a single color, makes it easy for viewers to see which data is bigger.*
- *Make sure each color is distinct!*
- *Color sections gray if you do not have data from those areas.*
- *Use a key and label it so people know what each color stands for.*

There are many possible "right" ways to break the key down to numbers. For example, you could have broken it down by tens: zero, 1–10, 11–20, 21–30, and so on. Because we don't have any numbers above 20, we decided to count by fives.

Now get out your colored pencils or markers, either in rainbow colors or many shades of a single color. Make a list of which states need which color:

- 16–20 (Michigan, Wisconsin, New York, Indiana)
- 11–15 (Ohio, Washington, North Carolina)
- 6–10 (California, Nevada)
- 1–5 (Oregon, Illinois, South Carolina, Pennsylvania, Florida, North Dakota)
- none (all other states)

Download a blank U.S. map. (We got the one shown from *https://commons.wikimedia.org/wiki/File:Blank_US_map_borders _labels.svg*). Print two copies so you can practice first. For this map, we do not need to convert our data to percentages. We're just going to count. Write the number inside each state and color away!

Check your work against this checklist:

❏ Is there a title? (Yes)

❏ Do you know the total number of people surveyed? (Yes: 150)

❏ Do you know how and when the data was collected? (Yes: survey on October 11, 2017)

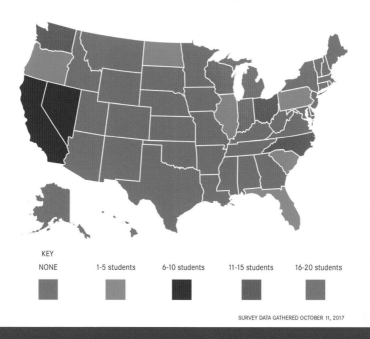

STATES WHERE STUDENTS IN OUR GRADE
WERE BORN (TOTAL 150 STUDENTS)

KEY

NONE | 1-5 students | 6-10 students | 11-15 students | 16-20 students

SURVEY DATA GATHERED OCTOBER 11, 2017

Does your chart look similar to this sample?

❏ Is there a color-coded key to the map? (Yes: shades of pink)

❏ Do the colors move in a sequence like a rainbow or dark to light? (Yes)

❏ Is there a color that represents "none"? (Yes)

CHAPTER 5

Bar Charts

Bar charts are made on a graph. In fact, they are sometimes called bar graphs! With a regular graph, you mark a dot for each location. Instead, bar charts draw a long, thin rectangle either up (if it's a positive number) or down (if it's a negative number).

On a graph, there is one line going horizontally (left to right) called the x-**axis**. There is another line going vertically (up and down) called the y-axis. Together, the two lines make a big plus sign. You have probably worked with graphs in math class. However, data visualizations don't always follow the same rules you use for graphs in math class!

Take a look at the example of U.S. military budgets, from Wikimedia, on page 26. Each axis is labeled. Study the labels. Along the x-axis, you see that every other bar is labeled with a

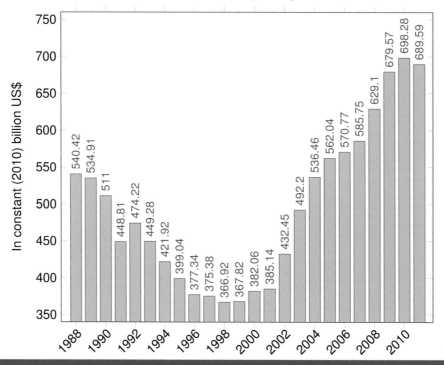

US military budget

Bar charts are good for showing how one thing changes over time.

year, such as 1998 and 2000. This means that the bar in between represents 1999. The y-axis is labeled as spending in billions of dollars. Now look at the first number on the y-axis (the one closest to the x-axis). In math class, the point where the y-axis meets the x-axis is always zero. But the y-axis here starts at 350. Because the label indicates dollars are measured in billions, the y-axis actually starts at $350 billion!

Wow! You can really see that military spending went way down in 1998 and 2000. This data stands out in a bar graph. You might not notice how big a change there was if you were just looking at a jumble of numbers.

Now let's make a bar chart of our own. We asked a homeroom of 35 students this survey question: "What hobbies do you have? Choose all that apply: sports, crafts, babysitting, texting, video games, reading." Here is the data we gathered: 5 students like babysitting, 15 like crafts, 20 like reading, 25 like video games, 27 like texting, and 30 like sports.

Wait a minute! Those add up to way more than 35 students. How did that happen? Well, it happened because we told students they could "choose all that apply." That means most of them chose more than one answer. It also means we cannot use a pie chart here.

Rules of Thumb for Bar Charts

Always check the y-axis for labels (like dollars) and **intervals** *(how far apart the number labels are) so you know what you are looking at. Don't assume the numbering will start at zero!*

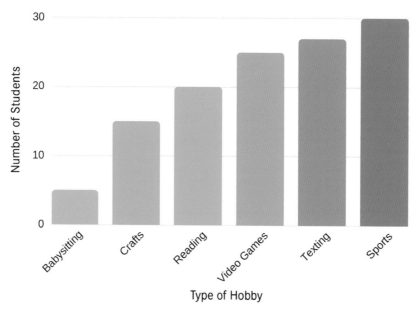

Answer to, "What hobbies do you have? Choose all that apply."

Survey of 35 sixth graders in homeroom 12: November 11, 2017

How does this example stack up against the checklist?

A bar chart is a good option in this case. Ask yourself, "What are we graphing here?" We need to show the hobbies and the number of students. Anytime you have data like this, it's easier to put the number on the y-axis and the category (type of hobby) on the x-axis. Sometimes, you'll see bar charts that go the other way, but they can be confusing.

Like before, let's draw a graph by hand. Here, you will notice that we use lines for each multiple of ten (10, 20, 30, and so on).

With bar charts, colors work a little differently. They don't have to be different from each other. It is up to you how you want them to look.

Okay, let's check our work on this one:

- ☐ Is there a title? (Yes)
- ☐ Is it clear that people could pick more than one answer? (Yes)
- ☐ Are the x-axis and y-axis labeled? (Yes: x-axis is "Type of hobby," and y-axis is "Number of students")
- ☐ Are the intervals labeled? (Yes: counting by ones)
- ☐ Is the number for each bar written either inside or above the bar? (Yes: above)
- ☐ Do we know how the data was collected? (Yes: survey)
- ☐ Do we know when the data was collected? (Yes: November 11, 2017)
- ☐ Do we know who and how many were surveyed? (Yes: 35 students in Homeroom 12)

Now you understand the basics of visualizing data. Maps, pie charts, and bar charts are three great basic visualization tools for your tool kit. Keep practicing! After you've mastered these simple types, you'll be ready to pull multiple visualizations together into a kind of data compilation called an infographic. Good luck!

Rules of Thumb

- Visualizing data should always enhance the meaning of the data.
- When you are organizing categories, sort them from smallest to largest or vice versa.
- Either use the same color for each bar or pick obviously different colors for each bar.

For More Information

BOOKS

Fontichiaro, Kristin. *Understanding and Creating Infographics*. Ann Arbor, MI: Cherry Lake Publishing, 2014.

Hoff, Tyler. *Understanding Data Visualizations*. Ann Arbor, MI: Cherry Lake Publishing, 2018.

WEB SITES

Beam—Chart Maker
https://venngage.com/beam
Check out this simple online tool for creating pie charts, graphs, and bar charts. You may still need to add some labels, but this will give you a great start!

Create a Graph
https://nces.ed.gov/nceskids/graphing/classic
Learn how to create graphs with these interactive activities.

GLOSSARY

axis (AK-sis) a line at the side, bottom, or top of a chart

bar chart (BAR CHAHRT) a visualization that uses long, skinny rectangles to show numbers

distinct (dih-STINKT) clearly different from other items

graph (GRAF) a diagram that shows the relationship between numbers of amounts

hieroglyphs (HYE-roh-glifs) pictures and other symbols that stand for words or ideas

infographic (in-foh-GRAF-ik) a visual document that combines many pieces of information, including visualizations, numbers, statistics, and words

intervals (IN-tur-vulz) spaces between objects

key (KEE) a section of a visualization that explains what its colors and symbols represent

pie chart (PYE CHAHRT) a round visualization with "slices" to represent different parts of the whole

INDEX

bar charts, 25–30

categories, 11, 12, 15, 16, 18, 28, 30
colors, 6, 14, 17, 18, 19–21, 22, 23, 29, 30

experiments, 10–11

government, 6, 12, 13

hieroglyphs, 9

infographics, 7, 29
intervals, 27, 29

keys, 6, 17, 19, 20, 22–23, 24

labels, 7, 14, 17, 18, 20, 22, 25–26, 27, 29

maps, 19–24
meaning, 7, 20, 30
message, 7, 11

Nightingale, Florence, 4, 6–7

percentages, 16–17, 18, 19, 20, 21, 23
pie charts, 14–18, 27

questions, 12–13, 21, 27

raw numbers, 16, 17

science, 10–11
social studies, 11
sources, 11, 12, 13, 17
surveys, 12–13, 22, 23, 27, 29

value, 7

Web sites, 12, 13

x-axis, 25, 26, 28, 29

y-axis, 25, 26, 27, 28, 29